[DAFFODIL]

[DAFFODIL]

CLYDE PHILLIP WACHSBERGER

AND THEODORE JAMES, JR.

PHOTOGRAPHS BY HARRY HARALAMBOU

HARRY N. ABRAMS, INC., PUBLISHERS

for Helen and Evelyn

EDITOR: Sharon AvRutick
DESIGNER: Helene Silverman
PRODUCTION MANAGER: Justine Keefe

Library of Congress Cataloging-in-Publication Data

Wachsberger, Clyde.
  Daffodil / Clyde Phillip Wachsberger and Theodore James, Jr.;
photographs by Harry Haralambou.
    p. cm.
Includes bibliographical references and index.
  ISBN 0-8109-5006-5 (hardcover)
1. Daffodils. I. James, Theodore. II. Haralambou, Harry. III. Title.

SB413.D12W33 2004
635.9'3434—dc22

2003020356

Printed and bound in China

10 9 8 7 6 5 4 3 2 1

Harry N. Abrams, Inc.
100 Fifth Avenue
New York, N.Y. 10011
www.abramsbooks.com

Abrams is a subsidiary of

LA MARTINIÈRE
GROUPE

WE ARE GRATEFUL TO BRENT AND BECKY HEATH, RICHARD AND ELISE HAVENS, NANCY R.
WILSON, AND JOHN REED, ALL BUSY DAFFODIL HYBRIDIZERS, FOR GENEROUSLY TAKING THE
TIME TO ANSWER QUESTIONS AND SHARE THEIR EXPERTISE. WE THANK JOHN LEE FOR HIS
KIND ASSISTANCE IN GETTING US STARTED.

PAGE 1: *N. ODORUS LINNAEUS*, SOMETIMES KNOWN AS 'CAMPERNELLI.' THIS DIVISION 13
DAFFODIL HAS TWO OR THREE INTENSELY FRAGRANT JONQUILLA-TYPE FLOWERS PER STEM.
PAGE 2: THE EPITOME OF SPRING, DAFFODILS ALONG A PICTURESQUE CANAL AT THE KEUKENHOF
GARDENS IN HOLLAND. OVERLEAF, CLOCKWISE FROM ABOVE LEFT: SANFORD KEMPNER PLANTED
THOUSANDS OF BULBS ALONG THIS SERPENTINE DRIVEWAY, AND HERE IS THE GLORIOUS SPRING
REWARD—AN INCOMPARABLY INVITING ENTRANCEWAY!; JAUNTY AND CHEERY, DAFFODILS
WELCOME SPRING AS NO OTHER FLOWER CAN; AN UNEXPECTED AND STRIKING COMBINATION,
DAFFODILS AND BAMBOO HAVE NATURALIZED ON THE GROUNDS OF LONG HOUSE RESERVE ON
NEW YORK'S LONG ISLAND; 'RIP VAN WINKLE' HAS UNUSUAL, RAGGED, POM-POM FLOWERS,
WHICH ALWAYS GET ATTENTION.

CONTENTS

Anatomy of the Daffodil

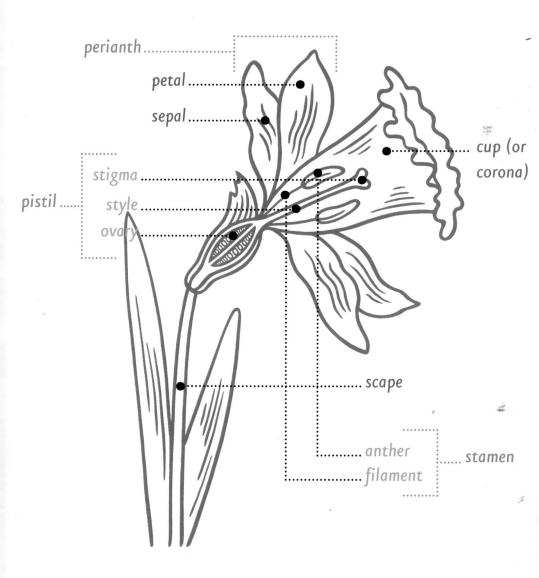

perianth

petal

sepal

stigma

pistil

style

ovary

cup (or corona)

scape

anther

filament

stamen

ILLUSTRATION: MEGAN CASH

OPPOSITE: UP CLOSE AND PERSONAL, THE DAFFODIL FLOWER SUGGESTS THE PRISTINE
MONUMENTALITY OF A GEORGIA O'KEEFFE PAINTING.

INTRODUCTION

THE CHEERY, stalwart, bright-yellow daffodil symbolizes spring as surely as do robins, scampering rabbits, and the first bees. These eloquent flowers basking in March sunshine instill hope in gardeners and poets alike. Shakespeare, in *The Winter's Tale*, speaks of "Daffodils that come before the swallows dare and take the winds of March with beauty." These familiar flowering bulbs thrive almost anywhere winters are cold and in almost any well-drained soil, undisturbed by rodents, deer, and most insects. Often their new foliage pushes up through the wintry earth and remains optimistically green during the darkest days, a promise of things to come. No garden should be without these early risers, heralds of the new season.

There are a host of daffodils—thousands, really—from diminutive grassy-leaved gems with flowers no bigger than a child's fingertips to jaunty giants sporting flowers the size and shape of an espresso cup and saucer. They bloom in colors from pure white through all the hues of yellow to bright orange, with accents of pastel pink, lime green, and even red. Sometimes a tall stem supports a single specimen; sometimes a cluster of small blossoms is a bouquet in itself. Many daffodils have clear, sweet fragrances unique to springtime. A vase full of these jolly flowers with their distinctive silhouettes will bring the colors and perfumes of spring indoors.

Scatter a few bulbs in special places around your garden. Each is a treasure to be anticipated through the winter and a reward to be enjoyed when the garden year begins anew.

THE JONQUILLA DAFFODIL 'DICKCISSEL' IS A VIGOROUS MULTIPLIER AND GENEROUS PRODUCER OF FRAGRANT FLOWERS, PERFECT FOR BOUQUETS. EVEN ONE STEM IN A BUD VASE WILL PERFUME A ROOM.

1 Daffodils in History

GREEK MYTHOLOGY relates the tale of Narkissos, a beautiful young man who fell in love with his own reflection in a mountain spring. In some versions he pines away at the water's edge until he is transformed into a flower, the familiar narcissus. Another version has Narkissos leaning far out over the water to embrace his own reflection, only to lose his balance and drown. As with most myths, the instructive message has endured through many centuries; our word *narcissist* refers to someone who is interested only in him- or herself.

We still sometimes use the name "narcissus" for the beautiful nodding flowers on slender stems which, growing by a pond or stream, seem to bend to admire their own reflections. But we also call them jonquils and daffodils. All these names are correct, but *Narcissus*, the Latin version of the original Greek name, is the official botanical name for all members of this genus of flowering bulbs. "Daffodil" is the common name and is the term recommended by the American Daffodil Society. It is properly used when referring to any plants in this genus.

Daffodils are native to the Mediterranean region, from the Iberian Peninsula (modern Portugal and Spain), east to Turkey, and along the North African coast from modern Morocco to the Middle East. Spain is home to the most species. The sweet-scented white N. *poeticus recurvus*, today known as 'Pheasant's Eye,' and the more strongly perfumed multi-flowered Tazetta types, including the Paperwhites, are probably indigenous to Greece and Italy. The Tazettas grow wild as far as Asia, but it is possible they were brought there through trade or migration.

Daffodils have long been admired and used medicinally and ritually. Ancient Egyptians used them in funeral wreaths. They were grown in ancient Greek gardens, sometimes in containers to be brought inside. In his comprehensive *Enquiry into Plants*, the fourth century BC Greek natural scientist Theophrastus, a gardener himself, offers instructions that can still be followed with success today on how to propagate daffodils both from seed and from bulbs.

LISA STAMM HAS CREATED A CHARMINGLY NOSTALGIC GARDEN WITH A CARPET OF MARSH MARIGOLDS AND DRIFTS OF THE WHITE POETICUS DAFFODIL 'ACTAEA'.

'HOLLAND SENSATION' PLANTED ALONGSIDE A POND CALLS TO MIND THE MYTH OF NARKISSOS, WHO FELL IN LOVE WITH HIS OWN REFLECTION AND WHOSE NAME HAS BECOME SYNONYMOUS WITH DAFFODIL.

The ancient Greeks believed that the sap of daffodils, and even their fragrance, had narcotic or stupefying properties. (The Greek word *narkoun* means "to benumb" and is the root of our word "narcotic" as well as "narcissus.") The daffodils known to the ancient world were the intensely fragrant types whose powerful scent, if not exactly stupefying, is too strong for some people's tastes today.

Daffodils were prized by the ancient Romans as well, both in their gardens and as indoor decorations for lavish entertainments. They were used in perfume, and because of their fragrance they were a popular addition to floral crowns, woven with roses, lilies, and larkspur. To supply these demands, they were grown in great quantity. Sales records of one grower in Roman Egypt, preserved on papyrus, include a letter from a well-to-do Roman lady requesting 2,000 narcissi for her son's wedding.

Beyond that, Romans considered the sap of the daffodil to be beneficial in healing wounds and used it on the battlefield. In fact the sap is an irritant containing sharp crystals of calcium oxalate. One wonders if the Roman soldiers complained to their doctors of painful side effects.

The Romans as well as the Greeks before them traveled extensively in the Middle East and Asia. Plants were traded regularly, so the daffodil became widely grown in ancient Turkish and Persian gardens. The wild *N. poeticus recurvus* was as cherished for its fragrance as the rose and was widely planted in Persian gardens, along with fragrant white and yellow narcissi.

In addition to enjoying the flowers for their beauty and fragrance, medieval Arabs used the juice of wild daffodils to cure baldness. As with the wounded Roman soldiers, one can only imagine the effect.

Throughout centuries of strife between Western Europe and the Arab countries, trade in new and rare exotic plants continued. When the Moors occupied Spain in the tenth century, they brought with them a taste for planting fragrant daffodils under flowering fruit trees inside enclosed gardens.

In the twelfth century, English naturalist Alexander Neckham, who eventually became herbalist to the king, wrote in his *De Naturis Rerum* that daffodils ought to be included in a proper English garden. By this time the flowers, which had probably been introduced by the Romans, were naturalized in fields and meadows throughout the British Isles;

there were many wild hybrids of all sizes and types, and they were beginning to attract the attention of scholars.

The British inherited the Romans' admiration for daffodils, and with it, apparently also their misconception relating to its medicinal use. John Gerard, an Elizabethan herbalist and surgeon who cultivated a physic garden at Holborn, prescribed daffodil extractions for ailments from coughs to acne in his 1597 *Herball or General Historie of Plants*.

In 1548 William Turner, the "father of English botany," had described the twenty-four known daffodils in *A Few Narcissus of Diverse Sortes*. John Parkinson catalogued ninety-four types in his *Paradisi in Sole: Paradisus Terrestris* in 1629, less than a century later.

Great Britain's Queen Anne, who reigned from 1665 to 1714, was especially fond of the yellow jonquil types of daffodil, and depicted them in her fine needlework and weaving. It is said that her love of this plant led her to establish Kensington Palace Gardens, the first public garden in England. 'Queen Anne's Double Narcissus' is named for her.

The earliest record of American-grown daffodils is on naturalist John Bartram's farm on the Schuylkill River near Philadelphia in the 1730s. Thomas Jefferson planted daffodils along paths at Monticello, and his friend William Hamilton, who sought out and collected unusual plants, grew Double daffodils that inspired envy in his fellow enthusiasts.

Daffodils were popularly known by many names: "daffodilly," "daffodowndil," "daffodowndilly," "daff-lilies," "affodyle," "chalice flower," "lent-lily," "lent-cock," "London pride," "eggs and butter," "sweet nancies," "pheasant's eye," "poet's narcissus," and "primrose peerless." With new varieties continually being developed all over Europe and Asia, some sort of official classification became necessary.

In 1753 the great Swedish botanist Carolus Linnaeus began to organize the then-known daffodils into eleven categories, which were of more use to botanists than to ordinary enthusiasts. In 1869 an Englishman by the name of Mr. J. G. Baker arranged the genus into three main subdivisions, anglicized into "long-nosed," "short-nosed," and "snub-nosed," and from these evolved the now-familiar terms "trumpet," "cup," and "saucer." With a few modifications this nomenclature received official approval at the first Daffodil Conference of the Royal Horticultural Society, held in London in 1884. A Narcissus and Tulip

Committee (now called the Daffodil and Tulip Committee) was formed and ruled that all recent varieties of daffodils would be given English names, with Latin titles being retained for the old species, subspecies, and wild hybrids.

Between 1840 and 1860 two English amateurs, William Backhouse, a banker in Darlington, and Edward Leeds, a stockbroker in Manchester, hybridized many unusual daffodils. Their interesting new seedlings encouraged further cultivation and crossing of daffodils. Some of the remarkable new cultivars were so desirable that a coterie of six wealthy English daffodil lovers began buying up all the bulbs of any exceptional new variety before they could escape into commerce, paying extravagant prices for sole ownership of the bulbs. One of the compacts of this club was that when members died, their bulbs would be distributed among the remaining members.

Of course many new cultivars did make their way into the market and into the gardens, and from there into the hearts of daffodil lovers. Hundreds of varieties were available to Victorian gardeners, and by the early 1900s daffodils were one of the most popular garden plants in America, a position they maintain today. Catalogues of that day listed hundreds of varieties, many for 25 cents or 50 cents the dozen. But there are others offered at $1 or more apiece, and the price tag of 'Avalanche,' described as "a very elegant new seedling with broad petals of pure white, curving towards the trumpet which is long and straight and also of pure white," was $150. The highly touted 'Peter Barr,' reportedly the most beautiful white Trumpet daffodil yet raised, cost an extraordinary $250 per bulb at a time when Americans earned a few dollars a week!

Most new cultivars were bred in Europe. But by 1924 it was apparent that some imported bulbs were infected with the grubs of the narcissus-fly, and an embargo was placed on the importation of daffodil bulbs. A silver lining to this dark cloud was that Americans began breeding daffodils with great success in Virginia, in the Pacific Northwest, and on Long Island, New York. Before long, Americans began to export daffodil bulbs to Europe.

To catch up with these developments, the Maryland Daffodil Society was organized in 1922, and the American Daffodil Society was organized in 1955. The American Daffodil Society publishes *The Daffodil Journal* quarterly;

its goals include to create interest in growing daffodils, set standards for judging shows, promote research, provide information on daffodils in gardens and landscapes, and encourage the development of new cultivars.

Today, there are an estimated twenty-five thousand named cultivars of daffodils, and they are grown in all temperate climates. Where it is too hot, gardeners chill the bulbs in pots to encourage flowering. Where it is too cold, they are grown indoors in homes and greenhouses. Competitive gardeners grow daffodils for show throughout the world, and in many places daffodil festivals have become long-standing traditions. Gloucester, Virginia, hosts one of the most celebrated, which is not surprising since it is the home of Brent and Becky Heath's world-renowned daffodil nursery. The Heaths breed many of today's new cultivars, and their fields attract thousands of visitors every spring.

Wherever daffodils are growing, the sight of their blossoms clamoring in cool sunshine signifies the beginning of a new season of outdoor pleasure.

OPPOSITE, ABOVE: DAFFODILS ARE A SIMPLE AND APPROPRIATE PLANTING AROUND THIS RUSTIC 1823 CARRIAGE HOUSE. OPPOSITE, BELOW: THE MAGNIFICENTLY LANDSCAPED GROUNDS OF LONG HOUSE RESERVE ON LONG ISLAND'S SOUTH FORK ALSO SERVE AS OUTDOOR GALLERIES FOR EXHIBITIONS OF CONTEMPORARY SCULPTURE. A PLANTING OF DAFFODILS IS AN INTEREST-ING COUNTERPOINT TO THE MONUMENTAL HIGH-TECH SCULPTURE. ABOVE: 'WHITE LADY' IS A STUNNING BICOLOR DAFFODIL WITH A LUMINOUS YELLOW CUP.

2 Selecting Daffodils

CHOOSING PARTICULAR daffodils from the many thousands available might seem daunting, but the American Daffodil Society has made it easier by organizing them into thirteen divisions. In each of the first twelve the flowers are grouped by flower shape, generally based on the relative size of the cup (corona) and the petals (perianth). The thirteenth division includes species daffodils, believed to be wild or naturally occurring hybrids. In catalogues miniature daffodils are sometimes listed together for convenience even though the flower forms of these diminutive plants may be similar to larger daffodils in other official divisions. The new and very popular pink, peach, or rose-tinted daffodils are also sometimes assembled in an unofficial separate group, where their color portraits seem all the more seductive. In addition to these groupings, daffodils are often classified according to their bloom times: early, mid-season, and late. Occasionally a catalogue will list separately those daffodils that are most suitable for forcing indoors for winter fragrance and color.

When choosing daffodils for your garden, select the ones that most appeal to you based on their photographs or descriptions. Then check their hardiness zones and bloom times. Keep in mind that plants may behave differently in different climates. Most daffodils are hardy from Zones 5 to 8, but some are comfortable with the severe winters of Zone 3. From the thousands of varieties available, you will have no trouble finding an interesting selection of hardy, trouble-free daffodils perfectly suited to your garden.

'SCARLET GEM' (DIVISION 8) HAS BEEN A FAVORITE SINCE ITS INTRODUCTION IN 1910. ITS PERKY LITTLE FLOWERS HAVE PALE-YELLOW PETALS AND SMALL, DARK-ORANGE CUPS, AND THEY ARE OFFERED UP IN CLUSTERS ATOP TALL STEMS.

DIVISION I

Trumpet Daffodils

These bulbs produce one flower to a stem and are the largest flowers in the spring garden. As they mature they spread into a clump sporting many flowers. Trumpet daffodils' cups are at least as long as the petals, and often longer, resulting in an imposing, assertive presence in the garden. This division generally has the largest bulbs and is among the cold-hardiest, north to Zone 3; Trumpets are not the best choice for Zone 8 or warmer. The pronounced Trumpet silhouette epitomizes daffodils for many gardeners.

VARIETY	DESCRIPTION
'Arctic Gold'	14". Early to mid-season. Huge, bright-yellow, perfectly formed up-facing trumpets
'Bravoure'	16". Mid-season. Vivid bicolor with pure white petals presenting a long, straight, bright-yellow cup
'Holland Sensation'	20". Mid-season. Orange-yellow trumpet vivid against pure white petals
'King Alfred'	16". Early to mid-season. Famous, huge, all-yellow daffodil, perfectly formed petals around a jaunty cup
'Las Vegas'	18". Early to mid-season. Cream-colored petals show off a bright-yellow trumpet on a tall stem
'Lorikeet'	18". Mid-season. Large pale-yellow petals frame a flaring and frilled apricot-pink trumpet; long lasting
'Mount Hood'	16". Mid-season. Large ivory-white flowers at first tinged with yellow
'Rijnveld's Early Sensation'	14". One of the earliest all-yellow large Trumpets. Flowers withstand subfreezing temperatures
'Spellbinder'	16". Mid-season. Reverse bicolor: yellow petals around a green-tinted trumpet that matures to white

When 'King Alfred' was introduced in 1899 it immediately became known as the finest yellow Trumpet daffodil, a reputation it still enjoys. By 1907 it sold for $15 each when many daffodils were 25 cents a dozen. Because the true 'King Alfred' bulbs are today still slightly more expensive than others, around $2 each, less reputable purveyors sometimes sell other yellow daffodils under this name. These other daffodils may be beautiful in their own right, but try to order only bulbs offered as the genuine 'King Alfred.' They are well worth the money!

New hybrids bring white, orange, and pink to the Trumpet group, which is equally effective in natural-looking drifts and in the formal garden bed.

Get a head start on spring with the very early-blooming 'Rijnveld's Early Sensation.' In the south it may bloom in December!

THIS FAMOUS ALL-YELLOW DAFFODIL, 'KING ALFRED,' WAS INTRODUCED IN 1899, WHEN IT WAS RUMORED THAT ONE BULB MIGHT COST AS MUCH AS A WHOLE STREET OF HOUSES IN ENGLAND! BY 1907, IT WAS LISTED FOR $15 WHEN OTHER BULBS WERE 25 CENTS THE DOZEN.

DIVISION 2

LARGE CUP DAFFODILS

These bulbs produce one flower to a stem, eventually forming vigorous clumps. The cup is not as long as the petals, but is more than one-third their length. These are the daffodils most often seen in gardens, deservedly so because they are both jaunty and graceful, equally effective in flower beds or naturalized in large drifts, and elegant in bouquets. Hardy in Zones 3 to 8.

To the casual observer Large Cup daffodils often resemble the Trumpet daffodils of Division 1 and sometimes the Small Cup daffodils of Division 3. Except when growing flowers for juried shows, make your selections based entirely on your personal taste.

OPPOSITE: 'MOUNT HOOD' IS THE EPITOME OF A TRUMPET DAFFODIL IN WHITE! ITS BUDS MAY BE TINGED WITH YELLOW BUT THEY OPEN INTO THE LARGE IVORY FLOWER WITH A CLASSIC DIVISION 1 SILHOUETTE THAT HAS ENSURED THEIR POPULARITY SINCE 1938. ABOVE: 'SEROLA' (DIVISION 2) IS EXCELLENT AS A PERENNIALIZER AND EXTENDS THE DAFFODIL SEASON WITH LATE BLOOMS. A MASS OF ITS AMBER AND ORANGE SUNSET COLORS WILL LIGHT UP A HILLSIDE.

VARIETY	DESCRIPTION
'Ambergate'	14". Late. Amber petals surround a large deep-orange cup
'Carbineer'	17". Early. Broad golden-yellow petals; deeper yellow cup rimmed in bright orange
'Carlton'	16". Early to mid-season. Two-tone yellow with vanilla fragrance. Popular for perennializing
'Ceylon'	16". Early to mid-spring. Sunny yellow petals around a reddish-orange cup
'Delibes'	14". Early to mid-spring. Bright-yellow petals; shallow yellow cup with a broad orange edge
'Fortissimo'	18". Early to mid-season. Huge bright-yellow petals with deepest orange cup
'Kissproof'	18". Mid-season to late. Pale-yellow petals around a flat orange cup rimmed with crimson
'Pink Charm'	16". Early to mid-season. White petals; large ruffled ivory cup with a coral pink edge
'Roulette'	14". Mid-season. Large white petals; round, vivid yellow cup with a deep orange edge
'Scarlett O'Hara'	20". Early to mid-season. Yellow petals and deep reddish-orange cup
'Serola'	18". Mid-season. Bright golden-amber petals and deep reddish-orange cup; good perennializer

OPPOSITE, ABOVE: AS BRIGHT AS YELLOW-ON-YELLOW CAN BE, 'CARBINEER' REVS UP A NOTCH WITH VIVID ORANGE TRIM ON ITS CUP, AND IT GETS BRIGHTER AS THE DAYS GO BY! OPPOSITE, BELOW: 'DELIBES' HAS BEEN A POPULAR PERENNIALIZER FOR HALF A CENTURY. ITS WIDE, SHALLOW, DARK-YELLOW CUP IS FRINGED WITH A BRIGHT-ORANGE EDGE, VIVID AGAINST YELLOW PETALS.

DIVISION 3

Small Cup Daffodils

These bulbs produce one flower to a stem, spreading into graceful clumps. The cup is less than one-third the length of the petals. These bulbs generally are good candidates for naturalizing. Many in this group are deliciously fragrant. Hardy in Zones 3 to 8.

The beautiful daffodil cultivars in this group often give the impression that their broad petals are fastened together by a brightly colored button. Many of their cups are edged in vivid orange or red, a trait inherited from the N. *poeticus* daffodils in their ancestry. They are all striking when mixed in bouquets with Trumpet and Large Cup daffodils, adding a different silhouette and often a remarkably sweet perfume.

If you've planned an early spring display with 'Rijnveld's Early Sensation' Trumpet daffodils, plant the Small Cup 'After All' to extend the season with its very late bloom.

VARIETY	DESCRIPTION
'After All'	16". Very late. Ivory petals with pale-yellow cup rimmed in red
'Barrett Browning'	16". Early to mid-season. White petals; bright-orange frilled cup with a pale yellow halo
'Dreamlight'	16". Late. White petals, flat green-tinted cup edged in bright orange with a deeper green center
'Edna Earl'	14". Mid-season. Large white petals; small dark-yellow cup with deep-orange edges; fragrant and good for naturalizing
'La Traviata'	15". Late. Silky, bright-yellow petals around an open cup vividly banded in reddish orange
'Mint Julep'	16". Late. Pale chartreuse-tinted rounded petals and a small green-centered yellow cup
'Polar Ice'	16". Mid-season to late. All-white heirloom with perfect petals around a tiny frilled cup
'Sabine Hay'	14". Mid-season to late. Round dark burnished-copper petals; small reddish-orange cup
'Sinopel'	18". Late. Pure white petals; small green-tinted cup edged in yellow; sweet fragrance

'AMOR' IS CONSIDERED A SMALL CUP DAFFODIL, BUT IT OFFERS UP HUGE WHITE CIRCLES AROUND WIDE, FLATTENED GOLD-AND-ORANGE CUPS, AN ASSERTIVE AND VIBRANT PRESENCE IN THE GARDEN.

DIVISION 4

DOUBLE DAFFODILS

These bulbs have either one or multiple flowers to a stem. The flowers are often shaped like full roses, gardenias, or peonies, resulting from the doubling or crumpling of the cup, petals, or both, and often there is variation even among flowers on the same plant. The effect is lush and romantic, and wonderful in vases. Some of these are hardy to as far north as Zone 3 but others are more tender. All are hardy to at least Zones 5 to 8.

This division contains some of the most lusciously scented daffodils. The flowers may be small and clustered, like a sprig of rosebuds, as with 'Abba' and 'Erlicheer,' or they may be large multi-petaled single blooms, as with 'Manly' and 'Golden Ducat.' Some are delicate and dainty.

VARIETY	DESCRIPTION
'Bridal Crown'	16". Early to mid-spring. Multiple blossoms of white and deep yellow; very sweetly fragrant
'Cheerfulness'	19". Late. Several small rosebud-like white flowers on each stem with yellow centers; sweet musk fragrance
'Delnashaugh'	18". Late. One flower per stem; large white overlapping petals around a cluster of apricot-pink crumpled segments
'Erlicheer'	12". Early to mid-season. Many florets per stem; double white with warm yellow throughout; intensely fragrant
'Golden Ducat'	16". Early to mid-season. Large, rich yellow double flowers with darker yellow cup segments
'Manly'	14". Mid-season to late. One sturdy flower per stem; pale yellow with mandarin orange segments
'Obdam'	18". Mid-season. Very double, almost pure white
'Tahiti'	16". Mid-season to late. One flower to a stem; soft yellow petals with flecks of reddish-orange in the center

ABOVE: THE ENORMOUS SHOWY FLOWERS OF 'TAHITI' COME ONE TO A STEM, WHICH IS PLENTY. THEY'RE SOFT YELLOW FLECKED WITH REDDISH ORANGE, EXOTIC AS THOSE TROPICAL FLOWERS USED IN LEIS. BELOW: 'ABBA' IS A DOUBLE DAFFODIL WITH A DELICIOUS SPICY FRAGRANCE. IT IS EASILY FORCED FOR WINTER BLOOM, SO YOU CAN ENJOY IT INDOORS FIRST BEFORE IT BLOOMS IN THE GARDEN!

DIVISION 5

TRIANDRUS DAFFODILS

These bulbs generally have at least two flowers to a stem. The flowers are small and nod gracefully downward, giving an elegant effect. Many are fragrant. They add charm to small flower arrangements and are popular in pots in cool greenhouses. Hardy in Zones 4 to 9.

'Thalia' is perhaps the best known of this group. Pure white and multi-flowered, it is sometimes known as the "Orchid Daffodil" for the exotic look of its graceful dangling blooms with flaring white petals. It has been deservedly popular since its introduction in 1916.

VARIETY	DESCRIPTION
'Fairy Chimes'	14". Mid-season to late. Up to six yellow blossoms per stem and several stems from a mature bulb
'Katie Heath'	15". Mid-season. Long-lasting white petals and pink cups on sturdy stems
'Petrel'	14". Mid-season to late. Up to seven small, pure-white nodding flowers per stem; remarkable fragrance
'Rippling Waters'	15". Mid-season. Ivory petals with yellow at the base of the crisp ivory cup
'Stint'	12". Mid-season. Jaunty, pastel-yellow petals surround a darker yellow wide-open cup
'Swift Current'	14". Mid-season to late. Pink bell-shaped cup with reflexed white petals
'Thalia'	16". Mid-season to late. "Orchid Daffodil"; gracefully flaring white petals; prominent, narrow white cup; two or three fragrant flowers per stem
'Tresamble'	14". Mid-season to late. Two or three pure white flowers per stem, each with a frilled cup and recurved petals
'Tuesday's Child'	14". Mid-season to late. Pure white flaring petals and long yellow cup; two or three flowers per stem
'World Class'	11". Late. Creamy yellow with narrow reflexed petals slightly darker than the cup; very floriferous and lightly fragrant

WITH AS MANY AS SIX CHARMING BLOSSOMS PER STEM, AND MANY STEMS FROM A MATURE BULB, 'FAIRY CHIMES' IS THE CLASSIC TRIANDRUS DAFFODIL: DELICATE AND ELEGANT, PERFECT FOR SMALL FLOWER ARRANGEMENTS.

DIVISION 6

Cyclamineus Daffodils

These bulbs have one flower to a stem. As the name suggests, the flowers have the windswept look of cyclamen blossoms, with the petals strongly reflexed back from the cup and the whole flower held at an angle to the stem. Despite their dainty look, they are entirely hardy and among the first daffodils to bloom. Hardy in Zones 4 to 9.

Plant these where they won't be overcrowded or overshadowed by larger emerging perennials, for example in open patches in the flower border or in a rock garden slope. Use them to fill in between small deciduous shrubs such as spirea 'Magic Carpet' or caryopteris 'Worcester Gold.' Wherever they are grown, their graceful stance and windblown silhouettes suggest wildness rather than formal plantings.

VARIETY	DESCRIPTION
'February Gold'	10". Early. Robust, floriferous grower with yellow petals and darker yellow cup
'February Silver'	9". Early. Ivory petals and cup with yellow tints; sturdy and long lasting
'Foundling'	10". Mid-season to late. Broad recurving white petals with a small pink cup
'Itzim'	10". Mid-season. Bright, assertive, long-lasting flowers; long, swept-back, vivid yellow petals around narrow dark-orange cup
'Jack Snipe'	8". Early to mid-season. Medium-sized flower with flaring white petals and prominent yellow cup
'Jetfire'	12". Early to mid-season. Prolific bloomer with reflexed yellow petals and reddish-orange cup
'Kaydee'	10". Mid-season. The pinkest Cyclamineus, with white petals and short, ruffled salmon-pink cup
'Peeping Tom'	14". Mid-season. Long-lasting all-yellow flower with strongly recurved petals and a prominent long cup
'Satellite'	12". Early. Extremely reflexed yellow petals; prominent orange cups with red rims
'Toby the First'	10". Very early. Ivory reflexed petals; narrow, pale-yellow cylindrical cup; very floriferous

AS ITS NAME SUGGESTS, 'FEBRUARY GOLD' BLOOMS EARLY AND IS ALL GOLD AND YELLOW. IT IS EXTREMELY FLORIFEROUS AND ROBUST, EVERYTHING YOU'D WANT IN A FLOWER THAT HAS TO BRAVE LATE WINTER'S BULLYING.

DIVISION 7

Jonquilla Daffodils

These bulbs have as many as five flowers per stem. The petals are spread wide and flare around the cup. Most are sweetly fragrant. These daffodils prefer warmer gardens where summers are hot, even into Zone 9, but they are hardy north to Zone 5.

These smaller daffodils add old-fashioned charm to any garden. The foliage is reedlike and the stems are narrow, lending a soft, graceful appearance to the whole clump. The perky flowers dance and bob in the slightest breeze, emitting characteristically sweet scents. They are unsurpassed for fragrant bouquets.

VARIETY	DESCRIPTION
'Dickcissel'	14". Mid-season to late. Lemon-yellow flaring petals lighten to white; pale-yellow cup fades to white
'Fruit Cup'	12". Late. White petals with a tint of green around a pale-yellow trumpet that fades to white; fruity fragrance
'Hillstar'	16". Mid-season to late. Bright yellow petals with white halo around the cup; long, broad, buff cup with white edge
'Kedron'	15". Mid-season. Coppery yellow petals with a tint of orange where they join the vivid orange cups; deliciously fragrant
'Pappy George'	14". Mid-season. Two or three very fragrant cheery flowers per stem; bright amber-yellow flaring petals encircling a reddish-orange cup
'Pipit'	16". Mid-season. Two or three long-lasting flowers per stem; bright-yellow petals with a white halo around the cup, which is ivory with a white edge
'Pueblo'	14". Late. All white and very floriferous; delicious fragrance
'Stratosphere'	20". Late. Tall, with large coppery yellow petals framing a darker golden-orange cup; very fragrant
'Suzy'	16". Late. Bright-yellow petals; shallow orange cup; crisp, sweet fragrance. Fantastic in bouquets
'Sweetness'	14". Mid-season. All golden yellow; sweet scent

JONQUILLA DAFFODIL 'FRUIT CUP' IN THE FOREGROUND AND TRIANDRUS 'THALIA' IN THE BACKGROUND ARE PLANTED WITH CANDYTUFTS AND IRISES IN THIS CHARMING ROCK GARDEN.

DIVISION 8

TAZETTA DAFFODILS

These bulbs, the ones used most often for forcing indoors in winter, may produce as many as twenty small flowers to a stem. Each flower has spreading petals that do not curve back from the cup, and their fragrance is legendary. Some Tazettas are too tender for northern gardens, but many are happy as far north as Zone 5. Except to experts, many Tazettas look similar to the Jonquillas of Division 7, though the Tazettas usually have many more small flowers per stem.

VARIETY	DESCRIPTION
'Avalanche'	16". Early to mid-season. As many as twenty fragrant flowers per stem, the cup yellow against white petals
'Canarybird'	14". Mid-season to late. Bright-yellow petals around an orange-yellow cup; three to four flowers per stem with a sweet fragrance
'Cragford'	14". Early to mid-season. Round white flowers with yellow halos around the small, dark-orange cups; extremely fragrant. Popular for forcing indoors
'Falconet'	12". Mid-season. Golden-yellow petals frame wide-open, bright-orange cups, up to eight flowers per stem; sweet musky scent. Forces easily
'Geranium'	16". Mid-season to late. Large clusters of creamy white flowers with sunny orange cups emitting a powerful fresh scent
'Hoopoe'	18". Mid-season. Three or more flowers per stem, yellow petals forming a round saucer under the orange cup; very fragrant
'Martinette'	16". Early to mid-season. Many flowers per stem, bright-yellow petals around vivid orange cups; delicious fragrance
'Scarlet Gem'	16". Mid-season to late. Sunny yellow petals surround a flat, red-rimmed orange cup; tiny green center
'Silver Chimes'	14". Late. Delicate-looking white flowers, up to ten per stem

DIVISION 9

Poeticus Daffodils

These bulbs usually produce one flower per stem. The petals are pure white and the cup is flat and round, often with a green or yellow center and a narrow red rim. The distinct shape and delicate, translucent texture create the look of a fragile porcelain saucer. Most have a crisp, fresh fragrance. Hardy in Zones 3 to 7.

Many of these daffodils were introduced in the 1920s and '30s. Their ancestor is the famous wild 'Pheasant's Eye,' the N. *poeticus recurvus* native to the Mediterranean region.

There's a less-formal look to these daffodils, evoking the nostalgia of flowers pressed between the pages of books as keepsakes. Perfectly at home in flower beds, they are particularly appropriate in open woodlands, among small deciduous shrubs, or scattered on a rocky slope with heathers.

Plant crisp white-and-orange 'Geranium' (Division 8) near a path where you can enjoy its fresh perfume, and pick plenty for bouquets for the same reason.

VARIETY	DESCRIPTION
'Actaea'	16". Mid-season to late. Large flower; white petals encircle a small chartreuse-and-yellow cup rimmed in red
'Dactyl'	14". Late. Round, flat flower with pure white petals and a dark golden cup with green eye and dark red rim
'Milan'	18". Late. White pointed petals form a star around a small yellow cup accented in green and red
'Pheasant's Eye'	16". Very late. Flaring white petals are slightly recurved; small, vivid yellow cup edged in dark red; very fragrant. Also known as 'Old Pheasant Eye' and N. *poeticus recurvus*
'Unknown Poet'	13". Late. White petals form a saucer around the yellow cup with vivid green center and deep red rim
'Vienna Woods'	16". Late. Showy white petals; flat, all-red cup

DIVISION 10

Bulbocodium Daffodils

These little bulbs produce one small flower to a stem, but mature clumps have many flowering stems. The petals are little more than a fringe, while the cup is urn-shaped and prominent, inspiring the charming common name "Hoop Petticoat" for the Species *N. bulbocodium conspicuus*, from which the others have been hybridized (see Division 13). Zones 5 to 7.

These tiny plants, sometimes found in catalogues grouped with the miniatures, will get lost in a crowded flower bed unless carefully sited. Plant them near small nonspreading perennials or in open patches mulched with small pebbles. Another technique would be to overplant them with annuals, such as creeping verbena or nasturtiums, once the daffodil foliage has matured. They are also charming in small containers, either in the house or outside tucked into special spots around the garden.

VARIETY	DESCRIPTION
'Golden Bells'	8". Late. Golden yellow hoop petticoat–shaped flowers
'Greenlet'	12". Early to mid-season. Larger than usual white petals around a pale-yellow cup with dark-yellow frilled edge and tinted green at the base
'Kenellis'	6". Mid-season to late. Tiny white petals around a prominent yellow cup

Tiny *N. bulbocodium* conspicuus, the "Hoop Petticoat" daffodil, from which all Bulbocodium daffodils descend, will naturalize where happy in an acid soil.

DIVISION II

SPLIT CORONA DAFFODILS

These bulbs usually have one flower to a stem, with cups split into segments and spread back close to the petals, giving an exotic un-daffodil look. This division is sometimes subdivided into two groups: Collar daffodils (in which the segments of the cup are opposite the petal separations and the cup is often intricately frilled and whorled) and Papillon daffodils (whose cup segments alternate with the position of the petals). Most catalogues list both types of Split Corona daffodils together. Often bulb suppliers will offer collections of several different varieties of Split Corona daffodils, which provide flowers of many different shapes, textures, and colors, perfect for instant bouquets.

Split Coronas offer large blooms with an imposing presence, attention getters in the garden or in a vase. Best thought of as something quite different from the familiar daffodil with its characteristic silhouette, they are novelties, beautiful in their own right.

VARIETY	DESCRIPTION
'Cassata'	16". Early to mid-season. Large yellow cup folds back over white petals, then fades to creamy white
'Mary Gay Lirette'	16". Early to mid-spring. A sturdy grower; yellow cup turns to salmon, folded back against white petals
'Mondragon'	16". Mid-season. Large yellow pointed petals around a tangerine frilled cup; strong fragrance
'Palmares'	16". Mid-season to late. Ivory white petals around a lacy apricot-pink ruffled and split cup
'Printal'	16". Early to mid-season. White overlapping petals around a ruffled yellow cup
'Sorbet'	18". Mid-season to late. Pure white petals under a cup of frothy orange segments
'Tricollet'	16". Mid-season to late. Pure white petals and a three-part tangerine cup; a striking flower

THE HUGE WHITE SPLIT CORONA 'COLBLANC' LOOKS LIKE AN EXOTIC TROPICAL FLOWER, AND ITS FRUITY FRAGRANCE ADDS TO THE ILLUSION.

DIVISION 12

OTHER DAFFODILS

The American Daffodil Society describes these as "Daffodil cultivars which do not fit the definition of any other division." Catalogues sometimes omit this group or list some with miniatures or Division 13. Divisions 12 and 13 are usually found only in comprehensive bulb catalogues.

VARIETY	DESCRIPTION
'Bittern'	8". Early to mid-season. Two or three smallish flowers per stem, with recurved yellow petals around a short pumpkin-orange cup
'Canyon Wren'	14". Mid-season. Yellow rounded petals set off an orange wide-open cup; three to four flowers per stem; delicate scent
'Jumblie'	7". Early. Yellow petals flare back away from a narrow, light-orange cup
'Royal Tern'	10". Mid-season to late. Very small white petals and vivid tangerine-colored cups with yellow bases; two flowers per stem
'Tete-a-Tete'	6". Early. Usually two small flowers per stem. Yellow, with a long cylindrical darker cup held by a ring of pointed slightly recurved petals

DIVISION 13

SPECIES AND NATURALLY OCCURRING HYBRIDS

This category, in some catalogues listed as "daffodils distinguished by botanical name," comprises species daffodils found growing wild as well as naturally occurring hybrids. Some catalogues list selections from this group under other divisions, using the flower shape or the plant's ancestry as defining characteristics.

These are mostly small, dainty flowering plants, good in rock gardens or open patches, perhaps sited near an interesting rock or at a turn along a rustic path. Their wild natures and long histories make them popular in historic restoration gardens.

VARIETY	DESCRIPTION
N. *bulbocodium conspicuus*	6". Mid-season. This is the wild "Hoop Petticoat," with upturned bulbous yellow cups set in a fringe of tiny petals. Naturalizes easily
N. *canaliculatus*	6". Early to mid-season. Up to seven little sweetly fragrant flowers per stem, with white petals and yellow cups
N. *jonquilla*	8". Late. Considered the "true jonquil," with two or more deep-yellow flowers on each stem; very fragrant
N. *minor* var. *conspicuus*	8". Early. Twisty pale-yellow petals and long brighter yellow cup. Sometimes listed as N. *nanus* var. *lobularis*.
N. *minor pumilis plenus*	6". Early to mid-season. Unique, small, yellow pom-pom shaped flowers in great abundance, looking almost like dandelions
N. *obvallaris*	8". Early. Deep-yellow flowers of true trumpet shape; forces indoors easily
N. x *odorus flore pleno* (*plenus*)	10". Early. 'Queen Anne's Double Jonquil' sometimes has fully double roselike flowers, sometimes flat petals around a doubled cup. Very fragrant and a good naturalizer
N. *poeticus* var. *recurvus*	12". Very late. The true 'Pheasant's Eye,' with stark white petals flaring away from a small yellow cup with a red rim. Strong, fresh, spicy scent
N. *pseudonarcissus*	10". Early. The famous small yellow daffodil native to western Europe, beloved for centuries
N. *triandus albus*	6". Mid-season. Small, gracefully nodding, ivory-white flowers with yellow tints, the petals swept back from the small cups

Miniature Daffodils

These are bulbs that produce leaves and flowers no more than 6" tall.
This is not one of the thirteen official divisions; each of these flowers
has characteristics linking it to one of those divisions. For ease of
ordering, most catalogues list miniature daffodils separately, sometimes
noting the division to which they belong.

Some miniatures are extraordinarily fragrant for such little flowers.
All are best sited where there is no competition from vigorous spreading
perennials. They can be tucked into pockets of soil in rock walls or rock
gardens, between rustic paving stones, along paths with other edging
plants, or in small containers. An entirely miniature garden could be
created around a child's playhouse or even around a charming dog house.

Daffodils come in all sizes. This perfect Trumpet type is only as big as a fingertip.

VARIETY	DESCRIPTION
'Baby Moon'	6". Late. Small, round, bright-yellow flowers with flat cups emit a remarkably powerful and delicious fragrance. Division 7
'Bumble Bee'	5". Very early. Vigorous miniature bright-yellow Trumpet type with narrow petals forming a star at the base of the flared and frilly cup. Division 1
'Hawera'	6". Late. Tiny "shooting star" flowers, all yellow with narrow petals swept back from the small bell-shaped cup. Division 5
'Kidling'	4". Very late. Tiny all-yellow Jonquilla type, amazingly fragrant for its size. Division 7
'Little Gem'	5". Early. All-yellow classic Trumpet type in miniature; the cup slightly darker. Division 1
'Midget'	3". Early. Tiniest of all-yellow Trumpet daffodils; the petals are separate around the cup. Division 1
'Minnow'	6". Mid-season. As many as five fragrant flowers per stem, white or palest yellow petals and tiny yellow cups. Division 8
'Sundial'	5". Late. Tiny all-yellow flowers are powerfully scented, several to a stem. Division 7
'Sun Disc'	6". Very late. Round, overlapping sunny-yellow petals and small, flat cup a shade darker; sweet fragrance. Division 7

Red, Pink, and White Daffodils

Some catalogues unofficially group these popular flowers by color for ease of ordering. While its characteristic shape places each daffodil in one of the thirteen divisions, its flowers are distinguished by being entirely pristine white or by having cups in unusual hues of peach, apricot, pink, rose, or red. Descriptions of new cultivars veer toward the poetic and often suggest that copywriters for glossy plant catalogues might be wearing rose-colored glasses.

For centuries hybridizers have been trying to bring true red in generous proportions into the daffodil flower. The color does exist in nature in the narrow edging on the cups of Poeticus daffodils. Most likely the red will always be on the cup and not on the petals, but to find fault with that is like seeing the proverbial cup half empty instead of half full. Breeders have created phenomenally beautiful flowers, some with wide, reddish bands on the cup, some with cups described as entirely red. Usually this "red" is more orange. Recently breeders have been using pink daffodils (originally bred from orange-red parents) to try to achieve a red without orange undertones. Some of these hybrids are becoming available to the public from specialty growers. The catalogue photos of new varieties are often enhanced as much as publicity portraits of a trendy diva. Even with the best new daffodils, colors will vary from climate to climate and from soil type to soil type. Experiment, but don't be disappointed.

All-white gardens are popular nowadays. Jump-start an all-white garden in early spring with drifts of pure white daffodils of every size and shape, from early blooming to late blooming. The effect will be as enchanting by moonlight as it is on a sunny spring day.

'Pink Charm' and 'Salome,' both Large Cup daffodils, are extremely popular pink varieties, and 'Masada' is a stunning new Split Corona with a deep reddish-pink cup. Among the reds, 'Decoy' is a proven success and 'Amadeus' and 'Catalyst,' each with a vivid red-frilled cup, are available from specialty growers. Many white cultivars are readily available; among the purest whites are the Small Cup 'Cool White,' the bold Trumpet 'Denali,' and the elegant Large Cup 'Phoenician.'

OPPOSITE, ABOVE: The tiny but perfect yellow Trumpet daffodil 'Midget' at 3" tall is wonderful in small bud vases at each place setting around the dinner table.
OPPOSITE, BELOW: Small but vigorous, 'Tete-a-tete' makes 6" grassy clumps with many tiny bright- yellow flowers like so many spots of sunshine in the garden.

Fragrant Daffodils

Paperwhites come to mind when fragrant daffodils are mentioned. Their strong scents are not appealing to everyone, especially in an overheated room, windows shut against wintry weather, which is unfortunately where these little flowers on their tall, spindly stems are most frequently encountered. But many of the hardy garden daffodils are deliciously fragrant. Outdoors, their varied perfumes are a welcome addition to the fresh spring air.

Even daffodils not listed as fragrant have a distinctive scent, described as a "wet earthiness" by Louise Beebe Wilder in *The Fragrant Path*. Wilder says that by inhaling the scent of a daffodil, "your spirit will be transported to moist and greening pasture lands, or to gardens where the brown mould has lately swallowed the last of the snow."

But to the fragrant daffodils Wilder attributes perfumes as varied as magnolia, vanilla, ripe pear, cowslips, and musk. The scent of the famous 'Grand Soleil d'Or' is characterized as "a mingled essence of Pineapple, Orange and Banana."

All divisions of daffodils include some fragrant examples, but the Double, Triandrus, Jonquilla, Tazetta, and Poeticus types offer the most varied scents.

The popular Large Cup 'Carlton' has a vanilla fragrance, and in the same division 'Louise de Coligny' is famous for its fragrance. The Small Cup green-and-white 'Sinopel' is strongly scented, as is the Split Corona 'Mondragon.' All Jonquillas are deliciously perfumed, but in particular try 'Suzy' and 'Sweetness.' The Tazettas 'Cragford' and 'Geranium' are justly legendary for their fragrance, as are the Double 'Erlicheer,' the Triandrus 'Thalia,' and the Poeticus 'Cantabile.'

OPPOSITE, ABOVE: Two of the world's most popular daffodils, Division 2 white-and-yellow 'Ice Follies' and all-yellow 'Carlton,' are paired to provide a colorful spring setting for a garden statue. OPPOSITE, BELOW: Tall and elegant, Jonquilla 'Suzy' is endowed with a crisp, sweet scent. Its bright yellow-and-orange flowers are fabulous in bouquets by themselves or in mixed company.

Daffodils for Forcing Indoors

These bulbs, often referred to as Paperwhites, belong to the Tazetta group, Division 8. They are usually too tender for growing outdoors in northern gardens, and do not require a cold treatment to flower. They are characterized by multiple small blooms on slender stems and an intense fragrance, which some people find unpleasant.

VARIETY	DESCRIPTION
'Bethlehem'	12". Ivory white petals with bright-yellow cups; fragrance considered the least overpowering of the group
'Galilee'	14". Pure white multiple flowers per stem; delicate scent
'Grand Soleil d'Or'	14". Yellow petals around an orange cup; pleasant, fruity fragrance
'Israel'	20". Ivory petals with small yellow cups; light fragrance
'Nazareth'	12". Pale green off-white petals around a chartreuse cup; mildly musk scented
N. tazetta ss. lacticolor	16". Silver white petals around a yellow cup; pleasing scent
'Ziva'	18". Prolific early bloomer with many clusters of pure-white flowers; spicy scent

Tender Paperwhites forced into fragrant early bloom have been cheering up winter parlors since Victorian times and may have been enjoyed by the ancient Greeks!

3 Growing Daffodils

DAFFODILS ARE easily grown throughout the temperate zones of both the Northern and Southern hemispheres. They do require a cold winter with some frost, but in warmer climates this can be faked by chilling the bulbs in a refrigerator. Most types are hardy outdoors from Zones 3 to 8. General planting and growing techniques can be followed throughout North America with local variations.

Catalogues begin offering daffodil bulbs long before planting time, often at early-bird discounts. No matter when you order your bulbs, they will be sent at the appropriate time for planting. Local garden centers always have daffodil bulbs ready at planting time for gardeners who didn't order them in advance or who just cannot resist a few more, but selections will be limited.

Start planning your daffodil plantings in early fall (or late summer in the colder zones). You should have your bulbs by October, or earlier in areas where the ground may freeze early. Once planted, daffodils require little care and will offer years of exuberant flowering.

GETTING STARTED

The first step is to check your bulbs for any sign of damage. Generally the daffodil bulbs sold in this country are healthy, viable, and free of disease. The large bulbs of the Trumpet, Large Cup, certain Small Cup, certain Double, and Split Corona types are about the size and shape of kitchen onions, and have a similar dry papery skin. The smaller bulbs of the Jonquilla, Triandrus, and some Tazetta types may be the size of small onions or shallots. The Miniature and some Species types have very tiny bulbs, no bigger than a clove of garlic. In all cases, the bulbs should be firm and dry without any breaks, cuts, or rot. If a bulb is damaged in any way, discard it.

It will be apparent that there are dry roots on one end of the bulb and the remains of last season's flower stalk, called the nose, at the

55

opposite end. The root end is the base of the bulb, which at planting time is the end that will sit on the bottom of the hole. The nose will point up toward you.

Like other commodities, daffodil bulbs come in different grades. The largest, most mature bulbs are categorized as #1 grade. A #1 grade bulb will have at least three younger bulbs, called offsets, clustered around it, each with a nose. This means each of the offsets as well as the central mature bulb will produce a flowering stalk. The effect the spring after planting will be of a small clump of daffodils.

#2 grade bulbs will have at least two noses, one on a mature bulb and one on an offset. The spring after planting there will be at least two flowering stalks.

#3 grade bulbs usually have one nose. These less-expensive bulbs are sometimes listed in catalogues as "landscape" bulbs, or are suggested for naturalizing.

All daffodil bulbs begin to multiply once they are happily planted. #3 grade bulbs should become #2 grade after one season, and so on. You will be amply rewarded by any daffodil bulbs you plant, as long as they are healthy to begin with and you follow a few simple steps when planting them.

SELECTING A SITE

The most important factor in selecting a site for daffodils is sun. They require at least six hours of sunlight each day during the growing season. This stipulation is less restricting than it might seem because garden areas shaded by deciduous trees in summer are often sunny enough in late winter and spring to allow daffodils to thrive.

Most well-drained soils are suitable. Although daffodils want plenty of water while they are growing and in bloom, they dislike sitting in wet earth when dormant. A sloped lawn area or raised bed that is only occasionally watered from June through the summer and fall is ideal.

Daffodils can happily naturalize in lawns, but since you must not cut the foliage until it has died back, a neatly manicured lawn is not the place for them.

PREPARING THE SOIL

If you happen to be lucky enough to have a sloped area in your garden and if the soil is workable, you may not need to do anything except plant your bulbs. However, the more you enrich the soil and the better the drainage you provide, the more you will encourage vigorous growth.

Daffodils thrive in a loamy, sandy soil enriched with organic matter. If your other garden plants are growing healthily, chances are your soil is fine. But if your soil is compacted heavy clay, if water stands in puddles long after a rain, if the surface cracks in dry weather, if grass struggles in the lawn, you will need to prepare the bed before planting. You should do this time-consuming chore well in advance of planting time.

One way to solve many problems at once is to raise the planting area a few inches or more with new topsoil mixed with rotted manure, humus, and garden sand. The coarse sand will not decay with the organic matter and will keep the soil loose, prevent it from compacting, and help the soil to drain better. Do not use beach sand, which may contain harmful salts. Work well-composted organic material into the mix. Packaged mulches such as pine bark also can lighten the soil and improve drainage. Raise the soil level in the center of the bed at least a few inches above the perimeter, so that you have a gentle slope in all directions, creating a berm with workable soil and excellent drainage. Keep the bed weed-free by applying a deep mulch over the plantings.

If you are planting many bulbs in a lawn for naturalizing and cannot raise the whole area into a berm, cover it with an inch or two of manure, humus, and compost. Grass will work its way up through this layer of top-dressing.

If you invest in just a few expensive new cultivars or rare novelties, it is worth taking the time to prepare each planting hole. A couple of inches of coarse gravel can be worked into the bottom of the hole an inch or two below where the roots of the bulb will rest, and a loose, friable mixture of topsoil, compost, and humus can be sifted by hand into the hole around the bulb. You may want to mark and label these special plantings.

57

OVERLEAF, ABOVE LEFT: WHITE MAY NOT BE WHAT FIRST COMES TO MIND WHEN YOU THINK OF DAFFODILS, BUT THE MANY WHITE AND WHITE BICOLOR VARIETIES ARE STUNNING WHEN PLANTED EN MASSE. OVERLEAF, BELOW LEFT: THE RUSTIC BRICKWORK OF THIS ENTRANCEWAY IS SOFTENED WITH PLANTINGS OF SCILLA AND MINIATURE DAFFODILS. OVERLEAF, RIGHT: GRACEFUL AND DAINTY, ALL-YELLOW 'APRIL TEARS' IS A CHARMING LITTLE PLANT FOR A SPECIAL NOOK IN A WOODLAND GARDEN.

PLANTING

Except for the thrill of seeing your daffodils in full bloom the following spring and for many springs after that, planting is probably the most enjoyable and satisfying step in the process of growing daffodils.

First, decide whether you would like small groupings of daffodils scattered here and there, or big drifts of many flowers. Then position a few bulbs on the prepared ground, separated by a distance of about three times their width. Keep in mind that each bulb will eventually become its own clump, so do not plant them too closely. (A patient gardener will plant them further apart than the recommended distance; in a couple of seasons the clumps will have spread close together.) But don't worry: bulbs can be dug up and moved if you, or they, are not happy with their placement.

A simple hand trowel is the best tool for planting a few bulbs here and there between established perennials throughout an existing garden bed. Choose a sturdy trowel that will survive the stress on its handle. For planting many bulbs in a newly prepared bed, a strong, well-made bulb planter is recommended. There are several variations on this tool, but the basic design consists of a hollow cylindrical digging blade that will pull out a plug of earth just the right size for a medium or large bulb. Planters with long handles are stronger and easier to use. Small hand-held bulb planters are often cheaply made and won't last more than a few holes. For planting a great number of bulbs in drifts throughout a lawn or in other unprepared ground, use a strong, long-handled spade. Or try a "naturalizing tool," an excellent tool with a narrow spade-like blade and a cross bar on which you can rest your foot for leverage when digging.

Generally the large bulbs of Trumpet, Large Cup, Double, and Split Corona daffodils should be planted at a depth of three to four times their height. If for any reason you cannot dig that deeply, you can top-dress the bulbs to the required depth by laying on a worked mixture of top soil and humus, and finish that off with a layer of mulch. In either case, fill in the holes with rich soil to the level of the surrounding ground.

The slightly smaller bulbs of Small Cup, Triandrus, Cyclamineus, Jonquilla, Tazetta, and Poeticus types should be planted from 3 to 6" deep, depending on the size of the bulb, or at a depth about three times the height of the bulb.

The very small bulbs of Miniature and some Species daffodils should be carefully planted 2 or 3" deep and marked or mulched so that they will not be disturbed during weeding or cultivating, as they are so much closer to the surface than other bulbs.

Whichever size bulb you are working with, set one bulb in each hole. Make sure the root end is sitting firmly on the bottom with the nose pointing up. Fill the hole in carefully without knocking the bulb over. A daffodil bulb planted upside down will eventually right itself and flower, but life will be easier for it if it is planted correctly.

If your soil is adequate it is not necessary to fertilize any daffodil bulbs at planting time. A top-dressing of enriched compost over the planting area is beneficial but not required. The old standby of sprinkling bone meal into the hole before setting the bulb is no longer recommended. There are fewer nutrients in bone meal than was once thought, or perhaps new sterilizing techniques remove all the benefits. Beyond that, bone meal tends to attract animals that might dig up the bulbs to get at the fertilizer. Any other fertilizer placed in the bottom of the hole may burn the new roots. Regular watering plus cool nighttime temperatures are all that is needed to start the new bulbs growing.

Local frost dates and average yearly rainfall will govern the planting and growing techniques for your own garden. Generally speaking, the coastal northeastern and northwestern United States, the mid-Atlantic area, and the central states have excellent climates for most daffodils, with long growing seasons and adequate rainfall. The bulbs will prosper with little additional care in these areas, as long as they are planted after the ground temperature has fallen below 60° F and well before the ground freezes.

In the northern states and southern Canada, early planting and watering after planting is important to ensure root growth before the ground freezes. Mulch deeply for at least the first season after planting to protect the bulbs. Choose the most cold-hardy varieties; more tender types may thrive in these regions in protected microclimates or be grown in containers indoors.

FERTILIZING

Daffodils do not necessarily require any fertilizer, as long as the soil in which they grow is healthy and fertile. Bulbs that have naturalized in meadows and parks get no help yet persist and thrive for generations. However in a garden, where they often compete with nearby perennials and shrubs and even trees, the nutrients in the earth get used up. Garden plantings will benefit from regular fertilizing.

The best and simplest method is a top-dressing of rich organic materials in late fall. Compost, packaged rotted manure, humus, or even a thick layer of chopped autumn leaves is beneficial. If the bed is kept mulched with bark chips or cocoa shells or similar material, these substances will continually decompose and enrich the soil.

There are a number of packaged bulb fertilizers available at garden centers. These can be applied in late fall or early spring, once the foliage emerges from the ground. Follow the instructions provided. There is no value in fertilizing again in late spring. The nutrients will probably not reach the bulbs' roots in time to be absorbed. Any fertilizer must be accompanied by adequate water to help the nutrients seep into the soil and eventually reach the roots of the bulbs.

PERENNIALIZING DAFFODILS

In the wild, only those daffodils that set seed truly naturalize. As the fertile seeds are dispersed, either by wind, rain, or animal activity, the daffodils' area gradually increases, following the contours of the land and the fertility of the soil and the available sunlight. The effect is always fluid and appropriate to the setting.

To achieve this effect with Species daffodils, you can let nature help you, but most hybrid daffodils will not set fertile seed in normal garden conditions. They will not truly "naturalize." They will, however, increase vigorously by producing bulb offsets and become long-lasting perennials, bringing color to a large area. When planting, try to imitate the overall shape and look of a naturalized patch of daffodils. Plan carefully to minimize labor and maximize floral impact. Space the bulbs generously to cover a larger area and to allow room for each to spread.

THE SPLIT CORONA daffodils are all exotic looking, suggesting tropical gardens more than chilly northern springtime flowerbeds.

Daffodils are spectacular in large drifts at the edge of deciduous woodlands, in sweeps throughout meadows or lawns that are not mowed in early spring, on rock-strewn slopes, and along sunny stream banks and riverbanks. They can be planted to weave in among large beds of ferns or between mass plantings of any hardy perennials, where they will contribute color in early spring.

The initial planting of a large number of bulbs is a major investment in time and money, but once it's completed the effect is priceless.

EXTENDING THE BLOOM SEASON

It is possible to have daffodils in bloom in your garden for many weeks, even months. Most catalogues offer an informative description, including bloom period, of each cultivar. Keep in mind that these indications will be affected by the climate and the hardiness zone in which you garden. Select one or two early-flowering cultivars, one or two that flower mid-season, and one or two that are late bloomers to extend the display in your garden.

And you can do more than this by getting to know your garden's microclimates. Where the snow disappears fastest might be the warmest spot. Plant some of the earliest-blooming varieties there. They will most likely bloom sooner there than elsewhere. Try planting a few of the latest-blooming daffodils in the coldest areas of your garden, where the snow takes the longest to melt. Their growth should be delayed a little longer. You might even want to try the same variety in different spots throughout the garden. Record the difference in blooming times, and use this information for future plantings.

Try using some or all of these methods to extend the bloom season. You may be able to have daffodils in bloom from October to May!

EARLY		LATE	
	'Dik Dik'		'After All'
	'Little Gem'		'Alabaster'
	'Perfect Spring'		'Cedar Hills'
	'Meadow Lake'		'Oakwood'
	'Rijnveld's Early Sensation'		'Peewee'
	'Sacajawea'		N. poeticus

ABOVE: GLOUCESTER, VIRGINIA, IS FAMOUS FOR ITS SPRING DAFFODIL FESTIVAL, AND BRENT AND BECKY HEATH'S FARM IS THE CROWN JEWEL. HERE, NEW DAFFODIL CULTIVARS ARE DEVELOPED FOR EVENTUAL WORLDWIDE SALE. BELOW: A YELLOW-ON-YELLOW CLASSIC TRUMPET DAFFODIL IN MINIATURE, 'LITTLE GEM' IS ONLY 5" TALL BUT STURDY ENOUGH TO BRAVE WINTER'S SNOWS.

CARE AND MAINTENANCE

Once you have planted your bulbs and watered them, the cool fall weather and the fertile soil of their new home will trigger growth. First roots will begin anchoring the bulbs in their new location and bringing in new nourishment. Then foliage will start to push up through the soil, sometimes even before winter sets in. New foliage can easily withstand even bitterly cold temperatures. The only possible damage might arise from a severe frost well after the flowers have opened; it could blemish the flower petals. The bulbs themselves will not suffer. As long as their foliage is allowed to grow and ripen and they receive adequate sunlight and water during the growing season, daffodils will thrive for generations.

There is, however, one concern: Daffodil foliage must be allowed to ripen, to live out its natural life. There is no need to pretend that the foliage of daffodils is attractive once it starts to fade. It is not. The long, slender leaves continue to lengthen and flop ungracefully as they yellow. They fall every which way, often on top of neighboring plants. Some gardeners, overly concerned with neatness, find this unacceptable. They chop the foliage off too early or gather up each bulb's long leaves into a bundle and braid or tie them together. This is incredibly labor-intensive and the result is no more sightly. In fact, bunching all the foliage tightly inhibits air circulation and encourages rot. If nothing else, the artificial hummocks are ridiculous-looking indications that someone's time might have been better spent.

A more successful and effective method is to plant small perennials nearby. Tuck the unsightly remains of daffodil leaves under the foliage of hostas, daylilies, hardy geraniums, or many other plants.

If the daffodils are growing in open patches in heavily mulched beds, fresh mulch can be sprinkled over the fading leaves.

At any rate, they can be pulled up or raked once they are yellow and dry or brown and rotting. In a natural setting, nothing need be done at all. The leaves will decay and return nutrients to the earth. This is perfectly fine for many gardeners.

WATERING

In areas with adequate rainfall, no additional watering is necessary for daffodils. During the bulbs' dormant period, from early summer through to fall, they need no water at all, but normal rains will not be harmful as long as the soil is well drained.

Starting in fall, when cooler nighttime temperatures encourage new growth in the bulbs, regular light watering might be necessary during dry periods. After the ground freezes, no further watering should be necessary until spring.

With the warmer days of spring, daffodils start to put on their major flush of growth, and regular watering becomes necessary for strong flower stems and well-formed flowers. Up to an inch of water a week is beneficial. Keep in mind that too much water is never good for the bulbs.

AFTER THE BLOOM IS OVER

With the hotter days of late spring, the blooms remaining in the garden will begin to fade. For aesthetic reasons, some gardeners deadhead (cut or break off the faded flower just below its base) their daffodils where that is feasible. In the case of daffodils that will set fertile seed, deadheading prevents seed formation and redirects energy to the bulb. In a natural setting, such as large drifts of many daffodils, deadheading is too time-consuming to be worth the effort. And drifts of Species daffodils or others that set seed should be allowed to do so to encourage naturalizing.

PESTS AND DISEASE

Daffodils are among the most disease-free plants you can grow, and because of their toxic sap they are distasteful to rodents, rabbits, and deer. In fact, some gardeners plant a ring of daffodil bulbs around plants favored by voles or rabbits, hoping to deter the pests.

If you purchase firm, unblemished bulbs and check for rot or mildew before you plant, chances are you will never have a problem with your daffodils.

If your bulbs do not come up in the spring, or if any foliage is yellow, speckled, or stunted, dig up the bulbs in question and discard them. They may have a fungal disease that causes rot, or they may have been infested by larvae of the narcissus bulb fly. These problems are exceedingly rare, and although they can be treated with commercial fungicides and pesticides, it is better to get rid of the bulbs. Put them in the trash, not the compost, to avoid spreading the problem. And avoid planting new daffodils in the same area.

MOVING DAFFODILS

Daffodil plantings can be left undisturbed for generations, but bulbs can be lifted if you want to divide the clumps or move them to a different setting. Do this after the foliage has ripened but before it has altogether disappeared.

Labeling the clumps while they are in bloom is time consuming, but well worth the effort. Depending on what will be most important to you in your new planting, indicate color, height, fragrance, or bloom season, or a combination. Don't imagine you will remember all this in a garden where several different daffodil cultivars grow side by side.

It is best to have the new site prepared before the bulbs are dug, so that they can be replanted immediately. Carefully dig first around and then under the existing bulbs with a clean, sturdy spade or fork. Try not to pierce or slice the bulbs. If you can remove a clump with a good amount of earth intact, set it down on a tarp or newspapers and shake off the soil while carefully pulling the clump apart into separate bulbs. If any bulbs are growing firmly attached, do not separate them. The goal is to preserve their surface and not disturb the roots more than necessary. Replant the bulbs quickly and water well.

If the bulbs must be held before replanting, keep them dry to prevent mildew or rot. They should rest on wire racks or hang in mesh bags where there is good air circulation, either from natural breezes or a fan. Labels should be kept with the bulbs.

It is best if the bulbs do not freeze before they are finally replanted. Treat them as you would new bulbs purchased from a supplier, except of course these have already become part of the family and you might want to be extra careful with them.

'BIRMA' (DIVISION 3) IS JAUNTY AND VIBRANT, WITH BIG YELLOW PETALS SURROUNDING SMALL, PERKY, ORANGE-AND-RED CUPS.

4 *Daffodils in the Landscape*

SINCE THEY provide one of the most beautiful of all spring flower displays, daffodils should be planted where they can be enjoyed from many vantage points. Wander around your property, in early spring if possible, noting which areas would be enlivened by sweeps of yellow or white. If the garden is large, imagine distant vistas of daffodils in great swaths that will draw the eye. Remembering that many daffodils are fragrant, picture them planted along frequently used paths or walkways where they will perfume the spring air as you pass. In a small garden, use them here and there among perennials and small shrubs to bring color and fragrance early in the growing season, and near entrances where they will welcome you home.

By their buoyant nature, daffodils lend themselves more to casual gardens and natural settings than to formal gardens. They are best planted in informal clusters and winding sweeps. Avoid planting them in straight lines or narrow rows bordering flower beds, where they will not show their grace and elegance.

A formal garden can be a fine setting for daffodils, however, if they are planted in a solid rectangular or circular mass. These plantings, sometimes seen around stately homes, are usually tended by a staff of gardeners who make sure the fading daffodils are quickly replaced with some other plant just coming into bloom. An expansive formal bed of spent daffodils is not a pretty sight.

Planted in loose groupings to imitate a natural stand, daffodils have no peer in the spring garden. If you have the room and can afford to buy fifty or more of one particular variety, plan on at least one large swath of the flowers. Site them where their bright, nodding heads will draw your attention toward a woods or a shrub-and-tree border. No matter how close your neighbors or how near the city, the sparkling expanse of yellow or white will evoke quiet woodlands and meadows and take your mind away from the rush of the modern world.

THE GULF STREAM'S WARM WATERS BLESS SCOTLAND'S LOGAN BOTANICAL GARDENS WITH A MILD CLIMATE. PALM TREES AND OTHER EXOTICS ARE SURPRISES AMID THE SHOW-STOPPING DAFFODIL DISPLAY.

However you plant your daffodils, make sure you can see some of them from inside the house. Often during their bloom season the weather is less than pleasant, and when viewed through the window of a cozy room the bright flowers can be a helpful reminder that warmer times are on the way.

EFFECTIVE COLOR COMBINATIONS

Daffodils, being predominantly yellow or predominantly white, blend well with all the other spring-blooming plants. Mixed with pastel hues, the effect is subtle and elegant. Mixed with bright colors, the effect can be cheery and vibrant. You needn't worry about clashing colors, no matter where you plant your bulbs. Color combinations are entirely a matter of individual taste anyway. What one viewer sees as a clash of colors, another may see as a hot combination. So use your imagination and remember that daffodil bulbs are easily moved. Still, chances are you'll be thrilled with the flowers exactly where they come up when you see them in spring.

There are certain spring-flowering plants whose colors contrast with or complement daffodils particularly well. All shades of blue set off and enliven the crisp whites and yellows of daffodils. Any of the varieties of grape hyacinth, or muscari, from pale azure to vivid deep blue, make fantastic carpets of bright color under the taller daffodils. Small electric-blue squills offer another stunning contrast for daffodils. From pure white 'Thalia' through vivid yellow 'King Alfred' to fiery two-tone orange 'Ambergate,' and all the pastel pink and peach daffodils as well, all will shine like sunny clouds over a carpet of blue. The paler blue of the little spring bulb puschkinia provides a gentler, more romantic, contrast. These various small spring-flowering bulbs, as well as low-growing common blue violets and true-blue primroses, are wonderful mixed in with the small daffodils and even some of the miniatures. Notice the blooming times of these plants in your area, and choose those that will be in bloom alongside the daffodils you have chosen.

OPPOSITE: LARGE CUP DAFFODIL 'MONAL' BLENDS WITH HYACINTHOIDES AND EARLY TULIPS TO CREATE A LOVELY SPRING WELCOME. OVERLEAF, CLOCKWISE FROM ABOVE LEFT: DAFFODILS AND TULIPS FORM A COLORFUL CARPET AT THE BASE OF THIS RIVER BIRCH; VIVID BLUE SCILLA IS A PERFECT COMPANION FOR ALL DAFFODILS; 'THALIA' IS SOMETIMES CALLED THE "ORCHID DAFFODIL" FOR ITS FLARING PETALS AND NARROW CUP; LANDSCAPE DESIGNER CONNIE CROSS BLENDS DIFFERENT DAFFODIL CULTIVARS BENEATH THIS FLOWERING ALMOND.

Lilac, purple, and mauve are also effective with daffodils. The graceful *Fritillaria meleagris*, sometimes called "checkerboard lily," dangles maroon-and-violet-patterned bell-shaped flowers on slender stems, a charming companion for the smaller daffodils like 'Jack Snipe,' 'Baby Moon,' and 'Sundial,' and stunning with all-white daffodils. *Lathyrus vernus*, spring vetchling, offers up clusters of sweet-pea–like flowers in violet or magenta above ferny foliage. And lilacs, in all their hues, are wonderful with daffodils, either on a flowering shrub or in a vase.

For a hot, sunny effect you might want to mix orange-and-yellow daffodil cultivars of differing hues. 'Ambergate,' 'Ceylon,' 'Delibes,' 'Fortissimo,' 'Kissproof,' 'Scarlett O'Hara,' and 'Serola' are each different enough to give subtle variation to a large drift. The overall picture would be stunning if contrasted by an edging of blue grape hyacinths.

Brilliant red is an excellent accent color in a bed of daffodils if a vibrant effect is called for. Tulips offer the widest range of red shades in spring. 'Red Riding Hood,' 'Red Emperor,' and *T. praestans* 'Fusilier' are among the brightest.

For softer combinations, pink hyacinths, such as 'Fondant' and 'Pink Pearl,' are especially lovely with white daffodils, or with any of the pink-cupped types. Pastel pink tulips, such as 'Montreux,' 'Peach Blossom,' and 'New Design' also lend a soft, romantic look. Frilly Double Cup and Split Corona pink-and-white daffodils, such as 'Rosy Cloud' and 'Replete,' are complemented by pink or white peony tulips such as 'Angelique,' 'Hermione,' and 'Mount Tacoma.'

For a jolt of color among the pastel shades, add a few deeper hues, such as vivid dark-lilac triumph tulip 'Passionale' and rich-rose peony tulip 'May Wonder.' Large groups all of the same cultivar, for instance the white-and-yellow 'Holland Sensation' or white 'Mount Hood,' make a stunning display. Alternatively, plant several different cultivars, each by itself in a small clump, throughout a varied bed among violets, primroses, pulmonaria, corydalis, and spring vetchling.

Grouping several different all-white daffodil cultivars can create an elegant tableau. Vary groups of 'Easter Moon,' 'Ice Follies,' 'Stainless,' and 'White Plume,' perhaps with the Small Cup 'Amy Linea' and the Triandrus 'Thalia,' underplanted with white grape hyacinths and white violets.

COMPANION PLANTINGS

Companion plantings are plants—bulbs, perennials, annuals, shrubs, or trees—that harmonize with and complement each other when grown together. When choosing companion plants for daffodils, find out if the site supplies all the requirements of soil, sunlight, and water necessary for each of the plants you are considering. Also determine if, in your area, the companion plants will be in leaf or in bloom at the same time as the daffodils. Sometimes the goal is to have a succession of different blooms in the same bed, in which case you could choose some plants that bloom early before the daffodils and many more that bloom afterward and continue on throughout the summer, perhaps interplanted with early, mid-season, and late daffodils.

EVERGREEN COMPANION PLANTS

Evergreen perennials can be especially effective as companion plants. They lend an attractive presence to the garden all year long, and are right there and ready as other plants come into flower and fade.

VARIETY	COLOR
Epimedium	white, yellow, lilac, orange
Geranium 'Biokova'	shell pink
Heuchera 'Autumn Bride'	white
Liriope	lilac, black berries
Luzula nivea (Snowy Woodrush)	white
Rohdea	white, red berries
Vinca	white, lilac

ABOVE: EARLY CYCLAMINEUS DAFFODIL 'FEBRUARY GOLD' BLOOMS BEFORE THE EARLIEST FLOWERING TREES. BELOW: BRILLIANT ORANGE *FRITILLARIA IMPERIALIS* IS AN IDEAL COMPANION BULB THAT WILL LIGHT UP A BED OF YELLOW DAFFODILS LIKE A TORCH. OPPOSITE: EARLY-BLOOMING RHODODENDRONS ARE JUST ONE OF MANY BROADLEAF EVERGREEN SHRUBS THAT MAKE EXCELLENT BACKDROPS FOR DAFFODIL PLANTINGS, AND ARE AMONG THE FEW THAT WILL BE IN FLOWER ALONG WITH THEM.

COMPANION SPRING BULBS

For colorful flowers in bloom at the same time as daffodils, other spring-flowering bulbs offer the most choices. Tulips probably come in more colors than any other flowering plant, but other spring flowers of various colors, shapes, and sizes—crocus, anemone, aconite, dwarf iris, snowdrops, fritillaria, camassia, brodiaea, ipheion, and allium—are also effective.

VARIETY	COLOR
EARLY TO MID-SEASON	
Chiondoxa	white, blue
Crocus	white, yellow, pastels, purple
Muscari	white, pale blue, vivid blue
Puschkinia	white, blue
Scilla siberica	vivid blue
Species tulips	red, many other colors
MID-SEASON TO LATE	
Allium	white, lilac
Camassia	white, blue-purple
Dutch iris	white, yellow, blue, purple
Dwarf iris	yellow, blue, purple
Fritillaria meleagris	purple, white
Hyacinth	pastels to dark red and purple
Hyacinthoides	pink, blue, white
Scilla hispanica	blue

GROWN IN A GREENHOUSE, DAFFODILS CAN BE PROTECTED FROM THE VAGARIES OF LATE-WINTER WEATHER. MINIATURE 'TETE-A-TETE' AND EXOTIC DOUBLE 'TAHITI' GREET THE SPRING.

PERENNIAL COMPANIONS

When choosing perennial companion plants you must think beyond coordinating bloom times and complementary colors. Some annuals might provide continual bloom of the same color all summer, but no perennial will. Beyond that, in different parts of the country bloom times will vary for different varieties of daffodils and perennials. In fact bloom times may vary even within the different microclimates of the same garden. Think instead of foliage texture and height, which will remain more constant. The varying shades of green, from almost yellow chartreuse to almost blue or even black, will also enhance the palette. Flowers, when they bloom, will bring additional color.

In the case of daffodils, another factor is choosing companion plants whose foliage will hide the unattractive fading leaves after the daffodil bloom is over. Among the perennials most frequently chosen for this purpose are the daylily (*Hemerocallis*), all the many varieties of hosta, ferns, astilbe, hardy geranium, heuchera, pulmonaria, tovara, monarda, salvia, saponaria, uvularia, peony, oriental poppy, and baptisia. Check out those that best suit your own garden.

VARIETY	COLOR
GROUNDCOVERS	
Asperula	white
Iberis	white
Lamium	white, pink
Laurentia	blue
Saponaria	pink
PERENNIALS	
Alyssum saxatile	yellow
Arabis	purple
Astilbe	white, rose, lilac, purple
Aubretia	purple, lilac, white
Brunnera	blue
Dicentra	white, rose
Ferns	shades of green
Hardy geranium	white, pastels, blue, magenta, purple
Helleborus orientalis	white, pastels, purple
Hemerocallis	yellow, orange, pastels, rose, red, lilac, purple
Heuchera	white
Mertensia virginica	blue
Primula	white, yellow, pastels, blue
Pulmonaria	blue and pink
Uvularia	yellow
Viola	white, rose, lilac, blue, purple

CHARMING DIMINUTIVE DAFFODILS ARE TUCKED IN AMONG TALL FERNS, CREATING A WONDER-
FUL NATURAL WOODSY EFFECT.

SHRUBS AND TREES AS COMPANIONS

Shrubs and trees provide the year-round structure of the garden, around and among which perennials, annuals, and flowering bulbs are planted for changing seasons of color and texture.

VARIETY	COLOR
SPRING-FLOWERING SHRUBS	
Abeliophyllum	white
Corylopsis	pale yellow
Forsythia	bright yellow
Lonicera	pale yellow
Quince	pastels, orange, rose
Spirea	white, pastel pink, bright rose
Viburnum bodnantense 'Dawn'	pink
SPRING-FLOWERING TREES	
Almond	pink
Apple	pink, white
Cherry	pink, rose
Halesia (Carolina Silverbells)	white, pink
Lilac	white, lilac, mauve, purple
Peach	white, pink
Pear	white

DAFFODILS MAKE WONDERFUL SPRING CONTAINER PLANTINGS, EITHER FORMAL OR RUSTIC. AN OLD WINE BARREL CAN BE THE IDEAL CHOICE TO DISPLAY THEIR CHEERY YELLOW BLOSSOMS.

5 Daffodils Indoors

ALL DAFFODILS are superb as cut flowers. For larger daffodils choose tall, heavy vases, as the flowers tend to be top-heavy. A massive bouquet of all the same cultivar in a sturdy earthenware jug will be simply stunning. Choose, for example, fifteen or twenty bright-yellow Trumpet 'King Alfred' or a dozen white Triandrus 'Thalia,' or try mixing variously colored daffodils of equal stature for a vivid, festive display in a simple glass vase. Pure whites such as the Trumpet 'Mount Hood' and solid yellows like the Trumpet 'Arctic Gold' blend well with any of the orange-yellow and orange-white bicolors.

Any daffodil can be displayed as a single flower in a slender vase. This would be a welcoming addition to a guestroom bedside table, especially if the flower is fragrant. Double 'Erlicheer' and the sprightly yellow-and-orange Jonquilla 'Suzy' each offer a perfumed bouquet on one stem. In England, however, one daffodil by itself is considered impolite, if not actually bad luck.

Daffodils highlight mixed bouquets with their neat silhouettes and clear colors. They enliven a bowl of lilacs, add stature to an arrangement of hyacinths, and contrast well with a few branches of witch hazel. When mixing daffodils with other cut flowers, remember to first keep them in a separate container for twenty-four hours. The sap that cut daffodil stems exude can shorten the vase life of other cut flowers. Change the water in the finished arrangement frequently to prolong the display.

CUTTING DAFFODILS

Choose only freshly bloomed flowers, or those in full bud. It is best to cut in the early morning or evening.

For most gardeners, daffodils simply picked and quickly placed in tapwater provide entirely rewarding bouquets, but professional daffodil growers recommend these steps to prolong the vase life of your flowers:

ALL DAFFODILS COMBINE WELL IN MIXED BOUQUETS, BRINGING THE COLORS AND FRAGRANCES OF SPRING INDOORS.

1) Cut or pick the stem as close to the ground as possible. If you are using a clipper, cut at a 45 degree angle so that the sides of the stem will not split. When picking, grasp the stem where it comes out of the ground and pull up and snap off at the same time. A clean break will help the daffodil stem retain moisture.

2) Hold the stem with the cut end up and the flower down. With the thumb and forefinger of your other hand, squeeze the stem gently and run your fingers steadily down it toward the flower. It might take a few attempts to get the hang of this, but it is worth learning, for it will extend the life of the cut flower by keeping the sap inside the stem longer.

3) Immediately place the cut stems in room temperature water. (If you're not going to be using them right away, refrigerate them.) Prolong vase life by frequently replacing the water, each time cutting the stem another quarter inch. Misting the petals with cool tapwater once a day will keep the flowers looking fresh.

Disregard the old tales about the benefits of adding an aspirin, sugar, or a few pennies to the vase water. Fresh tapwater is all that daffodils require.

FORCING DAFFODILS

Some varieties of daffodils are easily forced indoors for fragrant winter bloom. "Forcing" simply means causing the bulbs to bloom earlier indoors than they might outside. Some catalogues will list separately those daffodils most suitable for forcing.

The tender Paperwhites are the most popular for forcing, and the easiest, as they do not require a cold period. But many hardy daffodils can be forced for indoor bloom, or for bloom in regions where the winters are too warm. These must be given a cold period to induce flowering.

MANY SPRING BULBS CAN BE FORCED FOR EARLY BLOOM ALONGSIDE DAFFODILS. HERE MUSCARI AND *IRIS RETICULATA* EACH ADD A DIFFERENT COLOR AND SHAPE TO THE PICTURE.

Forcing Non-Hardy Paperwhites

These bulbs, mostly in the Tazetta group, are always available from mail-order catalogues and at appropriate times in local garden centers and even supermarkets. While famous for their fragrance, their strong scents are not pleasing to everyone. Some people would not dream of a winter or early spring without a bowl of Paperwhites in the house; others cannot bear to have them in the same room. See page 52 for a list of recommended varieties.

These bulbs can be grown in any small container, from a shallow terra-cotta pot to a decorative porcelain bowl. If they are grown in a simple flowerpot with a drainage hole, the whole thing can be set inside any larger, more decorative bowl or urn for special occasions.

When you receive your Paperwhite bulbs, store them in a warm place indoors until you plant them. Do not put them in the refrigerator or a cold garage.

Choose an appropriate size pot for the number of bulbs you will plant, considering the bulbs can be set quite closely, even touching. Place an inch-deep layer of coarse sand, fine gravel, or small pebbles on the bottom of the container, to help drainage. Some gardeners recommend adding a little charcoal to keep the water fresh. Fill the pot three-quarters full with a sterile coarse-textured potting soil mix or soil from your garden amended with peat moss, pine bark chips, and sand or fine gravel.

Arrange the bulbs in the container on the surface of the soil and fill in around them with a half-inch more of the soil mix. Add heavier pebbles around the bulbs to just below the rim of the container. The noses and some of the top part of the bulbs should still be exposed. While plain white pebbles or gravel in a simple ceramic bowl are traditional and give the most natural and charming old-fashioned look to a planting of Paperwhites, you could use colored pebbles, beach glass, or marbles, or other similar material for a decorative look.

Water well. Do not let the soil dry out, but do avoid standing water in the container or saucer. Keep in a warm, bright spot. Sun is beneficial during the initial growing period. Once the flowers bloom, move the arrangement whenever and wherever it is needed to brighten a corner of a room, but avoid direct sunlight to prolong the blooming period.

Forcing Hardy Daffodils

By forcing a few different varieties of daffodils in containers, and starting them at different times, you can have blooming plants indoors or in the greenhouse from late fall throughout the winter. The hardy daffodils that are timed to bloom in very early spring may be safely set outside in window boxes and containers even before the garden daffodils have bloomed, getting a jump-start on the season. Forced bulbs can even be set into the ground in their pots. For best results, choose bulbs that are listed as "easy forcers" or "reliable for forcing." If ordering from a catalogue, specify that you want the bulbs for forcing and will require them earlier than they are shipped for outdoor planting.

Hardy daffodil bulbs require an extended cold period at temperatures below freezing to induce flowering. The length of the cold period varies depending on the cultivar, but usually somewhere from twelve to sixteen weeks is recommended. If detailed instructions are not sent with the bulbs, you'll have to experiment, keeping in mind that smaller bulbs usually require a shorter period. Keeping bulbs cold longer will not harm them; it will only delay their bloom, which may be desirable if you want some very late flowers.

When you receive your bulbs store them loose and dry in your refrigerator (not freezer) for six to eight weeks. They can be kept in an onion bag for convenience—just don't confuse them! If you want blooms over a long period, remove the bulbs a few at a time so that you can stagger your plantings. Start potting the bulbs only after the outside soil temperature is at or below 60° and heading down. Of course, you must live in an area where the temperatures will eventually go below freezing.

Select containers appropriate for the size and number of the bulbs you intend to plant in each one. The container must be deep enough to hold the entire bulb below the surface of the soil, but the bulbs can be planted closely, even touching. Cover the drainage holes with pieces of broken pot to prevent spillage, and then put an inch or two of coarse sand, fine gravel, or small pebbles on the bottom of the pot, followed by an inch or two of sterile, coarse potting mix. If you prefer to use your own garden soil, mix in sand, perlite, or even bark chips. The mix must drain easily, or the bulbs will rot.

Arrange the bulbs on the surface of the soil and fill in with more soil to cover the bulbs completely. Water well and allow to drain.

Place the pots outside in an accessible area so you can check on their growth. Cover them deeply with mulch to protect them from thawing and freezing. You will not need to water them again unless there isn't normal rainfall or if you are in a typically dry region. If watering is necessary, do it sparingly just to prevent the soil from drying out.

After four weeks, check if any roots are growing out of the bottoms of the pots, signaling that growth has begun. Some cultivars will begin rooting earlier than others. Keep checking every few days over the next few weeks. Bring containers of rooting bulbs indoors or into a heated greenhouse.

The amount of warmth you provide will govern the speed at which the bulbs will leaf out and grow. More warmth will hasten earlier flowering. Here's an opportunity to experiment: place pots of the same cultivars in different situations, and see which bloom earliest. In a greenhouse, heating tapes or mats can provide additional heat. In the home, grow lights will hasten leaf growth, or simply keep the pots in the warmest room in the sunniest window. Sunlight is necessary for sturdy leaves and flower stalks. Consider alternating different pots in the sunniest window to slow some down and hasten others.

Once buds have formed, keep checking the surface of the soil for dryness, but water carefully. Overwatering can still rot the bulbs. As the daffodils come into flower, they can be used anywhere in the house in the same way as Paperwhites. Strong sunlight will fade the flowers, so keep them in indirect but bright light.

If the forced bulbs are meant for garden use, plant them outside after danger of severe frost. The entire pot can be set into the ground if the effect you seek is temporary, or the bulbs can be gently removed from the pot and planted in the garden, where they can remain for years.

OPPOSITE, ABOVE: THE SPLIT CORONA 'PRINTAL' HAS A RUFFLED YELLOW CUP NESTLED IN BIG WHITE PETALS, LIKE DELICIOUS LEMON SORBET ON A PORCELAIN PLATE. IT'S EARLY TO BLOOM AND LONG LASTING. OPPOSITE, BELOW: 'BARRETT BROWNING' WILL START THE SPRING ON A VIVID NOTE WITH ITS BRIGHT ORANGE, YELLOW, AND WHITE COMBINATION. IT IS A GOOD PERENNIALIZER, TOO, SO YOU CAN HAVE MASSES OF ITS BRILLIANT FLOWERS IN THE GARDEN AND IN BOUQUETS.

93

VARIETY	COLOR
HARDY DAFFODILS FOR FORCING	
'Barrett Browning' (Small Cup)	white petals with red-orange cup
'Bridal Crown' (Double)	ivory and yellow, very fragrant
N. *canaliculatus* (Species)	white petals with yellow cups
'Carlton' (Large Cup)	two-toned yellow, vanilla fragrance
'Cassata' (Split Corona)	white petals with broad, ruffled pale-yellow cup
'Cragford' (Tazetta)	white petals with orange cup, fragrant
'Dutch Master' (Trumpet)	yellow
'Early Bride' (Large Cup)	white petals with orange cup
'Erlicheer' (Double)	white and yellow, very fragrant
'February Gold' (Cyclamineus)	yellow petals with darker cup
'Foresight' (Trumpet)	white petals with yellow trumpet
'Garden Princess' (Cyclamineus)	yellow
'Geranium' (Tazetta)	white petals with orange cup, fragrant
'Hawera' (Miniature)	soft yellow
'Ice Follies' (Large Cup)	white petals with yellow cup
'Little Gem' (Miniature)	yellow petals and bright yellow cup
'Printal' (Split Corona)	white petals with frilly yellow and white cup
'Sweetness' (Jonquilla)	yellow, very fragrant
'Unsurpassable' (Trumpet)	yellow

SOURCES

VISIT THESE websites and order catalogues from the following nurseries. The websites and catalogues include many glorious color photographs, as well as growing information, which will help you make your selections.

BRENT AND BECKY'S BULBS
7463 Heath Tr.
Gloucester, VA 23061
(877) 661-2852
www.brentandbeckysbulbs.com

DUTCH GARDENS
144 Intervale Rd.
Burlington, VT 05401
(800) 944-2250
www.dutchgardens.com

GRANT E. MITSCH NOVELTY DAFFODILS
P.O. Box 218
Hubbard, OR 97032
(503) 651-2742
www.web-ster.com/havensr/mitsch

JOHN SCHEEPERS, INC.
23 Tulip Dr.
P. O. Box 638
Bantam, CT 06750-0638
(860) 567-0838
www.johnscheepers.com

McCLURE & ZIMMERMAN
108 W. Winnebago St.
P.O. Box 368
Friesland, WI 53935-0368
(800) 883-6988
www.mzbulb.com

NANCY R. WILSON
6525 Briceland-Thorn Rd.
Garberville, CA 95542
(707) 923-2407
www.asis.com/~nwilson

OAKWOOD DAFFODILS
2330 W. Bertrand Rd.
Niles, MI 49120
(269) 684-3327
e-mail: oakwooddaff@earthlink.net

VAN DYCK'S
P.O. Box 430
Brightwaters, NY 11718-0430
(800) 248-2852
www.vandycks.com

VAN ENGELEN INC.
23 Tulip Dr.
P.O. Box 638
Bantam, CT 06750
(860) 567-8734
www.vanengelen.com

WAYSIDE GARDENS
1 Garden Lane
Hodges, SC 29695-0001
(800) 845-1124
www.waysidegardens.com

INDEX